DOLPHINS: Our Friends in the Sea

Dolphins and Other Toothed Whales

by Judith E. Rinard

BOOKS FOR WORLD EXPLORERS
NATIONAL GEOGRAPHIC SOCIETY

CONTENTS

Copyright © 1986 National Geographic Society   Library of Congress CIP data: page 103

CHAPTER 1

HERE COME THE DOLPHINS!

Leaping high, five Pacific white-sided dolphins perform for a crowd at Sea World in San Diego, California.

■ *Meeting face to face. While feeding dolphins and other whales at San Diego's Sea World, visitors have a chance to pet them. Here, a Pacific white-sided dolphin, a pilot whale, and a bottlenose dolphin swim up for petting and treats. Their new friends are William Wilson, 13, and Janelle Berendes, 11, both of El Cajon, California; and Lori Sanderson, 11, on the right, of Titusville, Florida. "Feeding the whales is easy," says Janelle. "You just hold out some fish and they take it." Also in the pool are belugas, Pacific black whales, and young bottlenose dolphins—just a few of the many kinds of toothed whales.*

FLIP NICKLIN

■ *Whale of a hug. As Tara Miller, 9, hugs Shamu the killer whale during a show at Sea World, she gets a friendly kiss (left). "I put my arms in a circle, and he came right up," says Tara, of Encinitas, California. "He felt smooth and soft and wet. I wasn't even scared."*

■ *Leaping backward, killer whales Shamu and Kandu carry two trainers in a stunt called the "back dive" (right). It's based on the whales' natural behavior of breaching, or leaping.*

SEA WORLD PHOTO (ABOVE); FLIP NICKLIN (LEFT)

Whoosh! A sleek, black-and-white killer whale shoots out of the water. The crowd gasps at the animal's size. Nearly as long as a small bus, it weighs 5,000 pounds (2,268 kg)* and is still growing. Sharp teeth show clearly in enormous jaws. The whale leaps, twists, somersaults, and then—with a tremendous splash—crashes down. Finally, it eases its huge body out of the water next to a small child. As a trainer stands nearby, the great whale gently nuzzles the little girl's cheek. The crowd cheers.

This killer whale is Shamu, a star performer at Sea World in San Diego, California. Killer whales are powerful animals. They are actually dolphins, the largest members of the dolphin family.

In the wild, these animals are fierce hunters, which is how they got their name. In captivity, however, they are known for their gentleness.

How can such a huge, powerful animal be so tame with a little girl chosen from the audience?

"There's a bond of trust built up between the animals and the trainers," says Dan Blasko, director of training at Sea World. "The whales know and trust us because we work with them every day. They respond naturally to hugging. We just gradually condition them to do this with a child. It's perfectly safe—and a lot of fun for the audience."

Killer whales and other dolphins—as well as various other toothed whales—live and perform in marine parks around the world. They delight millions of people every year. Their natural home is the sea. Although they look like fish and are right at home in the water, they are warm-blooded, air-breathing mammals, just as cows, dogs, and people are. Whales must come to the surface regularly to breathe.

Toothed whales are members of a group of sea mammals called cetaceans (see-TAY-shuns). This name comes from a Greek word that means

*Metric figures in this book have been rounded off.

"whale." Whales are divided into two main groups: those with teeth, called toothed whales; and those without teeth, called baleen (buh-LEEN) whales.

The toothed whales most commonly seen in marine parks are Atlantic bottlenose dolphins. They were named long ago by sailors who thought their long slim snouts resembled bottles. These playful dolphins always appear to be smiling because of the way their mouths naturally curve.

Although dolphins have been kept in aquariums for more than a hundred years, formal training of these animals did not begin until the 1940s. Such training began at Marineland of Florida. At first, bottlenose dolphins were merely exhibited there with other sea animals. Late one night, an employee noticed that one of the dolphins seemed to be tossing a pelican feather toward him. The man picked up the feather and tossed it back. Soon, the dolphin was tossing him not only feathers, but also pebbles, inner tubes, and rubber balls. The shows we see today gradually developed as a result of this game.

Today, dolphins and other whales perform many crowd-pleasing stunts: leaping high and doing

■ *Up and over. Cindy and Diego, two Atlantic bottlenose dolphins, entertain the crowds by leaping over a hurdle at Sea World. These dolphins can jump as high as 20 feet (6 m). They also perform acrobatic leaps and spins. In the sea, dolphins breach often and take quick looks around.*

■ *"It takes teamwork and trust to do this," says trainer Joanne Webber. She perches on the nose of Shamu, as he lifts her out of the water. "Shamu is very gentle and helps me balance on his head before he comes up," she adds. This stunt was invented during play sessions. "The whales become very playful when we swim underwater with them," Joanne explains. She based this feat on the whales' habit of popping out of the ocean to look around. This behavior is called "spy hopping."*

flips, jumping over hurdles, playing with balls, walking on their tails, carrying trainers on fast rides, and performing graceful water ballets in unison.

How do trainers get dolphins to do these things? "We start out by building a friendship with the animals," explains trainer Dan Blasko. "We spend a lot of time touching them, rubbing them, and playing with them. We make sure they enjoy being with us. Then we gradually begin to teach them show behaviors. The show behaviors are extensions of the whales' natural habits."

For example, getting a killer whale to leap far out of the water makes use of the whale's natural leaping ability and its curiosity. A trainer stretches a rope across the pool. When the curious whale comes up and nudges the rope, it gets a fish as a reward. Gradually, the trainer raises the rope higher, and the whale begins to jump over it. Each time, the trainer rewards the whale with food, a rubdown, or praise. Before long, the audience is enjoying spectacular leaps in a show.

"We always use positive methods, never punishment," says Dan. "We just ignore anything wrong. We also vary the routines a lot so the animals don't become bored. They're very intelligent."

■ *Open wide! Joanne feeds Namu some squid for breakfast. Each day, a killer whale eats 200 pounds (91 kg) of food, including squid, mackerel, and salmon.*

Trainers do much more than teach the animals. In the course of a day, they also care for them in a variety of ways.

Joanne Webber works as a killer-whale trainer at Sea World in San Diego. When she arrives early in the day, the first thing she does is greet the animals and check to see how they are.

"When I arrive in the morning," says Joanne, "all the animals rush over. They're really glad to see me. I can tell how they're feeling by looking them in the eye. Their eyes are very expressive." If Joanne is worried about an animal, she will call a veterinarian.

Then she prepares breakfast for the whales. They get whopping servings of fresh squid and various kinds of fish with vitamin pills tucked in.

Joanne then gets into the water and begins a series of play, exercise, and learning sessions with the whales. Later that day, she and the whales will perform some of these same activities in a show.

What's the most rewarding thing about her job? "When you first start," says Joanne, "the animals like to see you coming because you bring food. After a while, though, it's *you* they (Continued on page 17)

■ *Taking Shamu's measurements helps trainers learn how much he's growing. As Joanne assures Shamu, Mark Beeler, in the water, and Jim Clarke measure his middle. Al Kelly records the information. The whales learn to slide out of their pool on command for regular checkups.*

■ *Leaping at sunset, two bottlenose dolphins play in a lagoon, a natural pool, in the Gulf of Mexico. This fenced-off part of the lagoon is used by the Dolphin Research Center, in Grassy Key, Florida. Here, newly collected dolphins receive care in a setting much like their natural home. Trainers spend months with the animals, slowly winning their trust and teaching them basic commands. Then the dolphins are flown to new homes in oceanariums all over the world. The center also breeds dolphins and studies dolphin behavior.*

■ *In his ocean home near the Bahama Islands, southeast of Florida, a wild spotted dolphin called Sandy swims with marine biologist Sylvia Earle (left). "He loved to play," she says. "He would gently mouth my arm and pull my hair, like a puppy."*

■ *Bottlenose dolphins often visit this out-of-the-way beach on Australia's west coast to play with bathers (right). Dolphins have come to this beach for 20 years, letting people stroke them on their sides and backs.*

(Continued from page 13) want to see. It's like working with your best friends."

Before oceanariums existed, people could observe dolphins only in the wild. To keep these animals from being harmed or disturbed, however, some countries now have passed laws to protect them. For example, it is illegal for anyone without a permit to approach a dolphin in United States territorial waters. Nevertheless, wild dolphins in various parts of the world sometimes delight divers and swimmers by coming right up to them.

In ancient Greece and Rome, for example, these animals fascinated people living near the Mediterranean Sea. Both the Greeks and the Romans decorated their plates, cups, and vases with dolphins. Dolphins often appeared on their coins, as well, just as eagles appear on some U. S. coins today.

In fact, the Greeks and the Romans thought of dolphins as sacred animals. They believed that dolphins were chariots of the gods, and they also believed that these animals saved shipwrecked people from drowning.

Ancient writings contain many stories of dolphins befriending people. For example, nearly two thousand years ago, a Roman scholar named Pliny the Younger wrote about a dolphin that played with children. It swam near the seaside town of Hippo, now Bizerte, in Tunisia, a country in northern Africa. The dolphin even allowed one boy to ride on its back.

In recent times, similar stories of meetings between dolphins and humans have been reported. One of the most famous tales involves a female dolphin named Opo. Read about her on pages 18–19.

Linda Erb has worked with dolphins for several years. She is the director of training at the Dolphin Research Center, in Grassy Key, Florida. She trains newly arrived dolphins and helps prepare them to perform in sea parks across the (Continued on page 20)

Opo, the Friendly Dolphin

Early in 1955, the people of a little seaside resort called Opononi, in New Zealand, noticed a dolphin in their harbor. At first, when boaters spotted its dark dorsal fin—its back fin—they thought the animal was a shark. Soon, however, they realized it was a bottlenose dolphin. Some thought the young female might be seeking companionship because she had lost her mother.

The dolphin seemed curious. She would swim up to the boats and dive under them. Someone discovered that she liked being scratched with an oar or a mop. Gradually, the dolphin began following the boats close in to the shore, where people were swimming.

They could see her in the shallow waters near the beach, waving her tail. She became known as Opo. People flocked to see her.

Opo visited the beach nearly every day and grew used to being petted. Although she was friendly with grown-ups, she seemed to prefer playing with children. She would swim up under some of them and give them rides.

Opo also invented games. When someone threw her a beach ball, she learned to toss it out of the water with the tip of her snout.

People still remember how Opo took part in an Opononi school picnic. The children formed a ring around the dolphin in the water. Then she swam around inside the ring and tossed a beach ball for her playmates.

The people loved Opo and wanted to protect her. In 1956, they passed a law making it illegal to harm her. Not long afterward, however, Opo disappeared. She was found dead, stranded on a nearby beach.

The townspeople of Opononi were deeply saddened. They buried Opo near the beach where she had given pleasure to so many. Then they covered her grave with flowers.

FEDERICO CASTELLUCCIO

(Continued from page 17)   country. Linda Erb also trains dolphins to work with scientists who are studying such things as animal communication.

"When dolphins are first brought here from the ocean, they're afraid of us," says Linda. "We start to build up their trust by feeding them and swimming with them. They seem impressed when we dive underwater and hold our breath the way *they* do. Later, we begin to teach them to respond to hand and whistle signals."

Linda says that working with dolphins is a challenge because they are so intelligent. They can easily become bored with routine.

"Sometimes," she adds, "they get tired of performing for us and want *us* to perform for *them!*

They love to see us clown around with buckets on our heads. They may bring us things to play with, such as rocks, and we try to juggle them. If they bring pieces of seaweed, we tie them in our hair. The dolphins enjoy this kind of play and interchange.

"Dolphins have different (Continued on page 25)

■ *A dolphin named Tursi and her trainer Linda Erb "hold hands" and go for a swim (right). "Tursi just offers me her flipper, and off we go!" says Linda.*

■ *Wriggling her fingers, Linda signals a dolphin named Nat to "clap hands," or move his flippers back and forth (below). When he does, she blows a whistle: "A-plus!"*

■ *A special kind of friendship. "Come here," Linda's open hands say to dolphins Tursi, Nat, and Delsey. "We're all old friends," says Linda of herself and the dolphins. "They are as curious about us as we are about them. Dolphins love reading our body language." These dolphins have worked with Linda for several years at the research center. "The greatest thing," says Linda, "is being able to enjoy the company of animals that normally live in the ocean— and to feel so close to them."*

23

(Continued from page 20)   personalities, just as people do," says Linda. Some are show-offs that seem to enjoy performing for crowds. Others are shy. They seem better suited to working on research tasks.

"We want these intelligent animals to enjoy whatever they do with us," says Linda. "We want to improve conditions for them in captivity, and we also want to learn as much as we can about them."

The Dolphin Research Center now has a large "family" of dolphins. Here and at some new homes for dolphins, such as The Living Seas Pavilion at EPCOT Center, in Orlando, Florida, experts are learning more about dolphins' habits and needs.

To see how dolphins and other toothed whales live in their natural environment, however, we must observe them in their home—the sea.

■ *Dog meets dolphin off Walker's Island, in the Florida Keys, as trainer Elaine Leslie plays with both of them (left). Dolphins newly collected for EPCOT Center, in Orlando, Florida, stayed here temporarily. Chae (KI), a trainer's dog, jumped right in with them. Below, Chae and a dolphin play a friendly game of tag.*

DAVID DOUBILET (BOTH)

CHAPTER 2

THE WORLD OF TOOTHED WHALES

While researching a film, Julia Whitty uses a hand scooter to keep up with fast-moving spotted dolphins near the Bahamas.

■ A pygmy (PIG-me) killer whale glides through the warm waters of the Pacific Ocean near Hawaii. This "little" whale measures only 9 feet (3 m) long. More than 65 species, or kinds, of toothed whales live in the world's oceans and rivers. Toothed whales range from warm tropical waters to ice-fringed polar seas. These animals are smooth and streamlined. Their sleek, torpedo-shaped bodies move easily through a vast, watery world.

■ *A pod, or group, of killer whales swims off the western coast of Canada (left). A pod may have 30 or more members, including young, called calves. The tall dorsal fin in the center of the group is characteristic of the adult male. The fin may grow to be 6 feet (2 m) tall.*

■ *A killer whale falls back into the ocean after breaching, or leaping out of the water (right). Whales probably breach to look around, to frighten prey, to shake off lice, or to play.*

Toothed whales make up a large and varied group of marine mammals. Besides dolphins and porpoises, several other small whales and one large one—the sperm whale—belong to this group. To see all these animals in their habitats, or natural homes, you would have to visit most of the world's oceans, several rivers, and even a lake in China.

Toothed whales in the wild live very different lives from the lives of their relatives in oceanariums. A good example is the killer whale, sometimes called the orca. Since 1964, when these animals were first put into aquariums, they have proved to be gentle and easily trained.

In the wild, however, killer whales are fierce hunters. They have no enemies except human beings. Killer whales do not hesitate to attack some kinds of sharks and eat them. Their diet also includes a variety of other fish, squid, and seabirds. Killer whales, as well as other members of their family—such as pygmy killer whales—eat mammals, too. They feed on seals, other dolphins, and large whales.

Killer whales hunt in packs. When attacking a large blue whale, for example, as many as 40 killer whales encircle their prey and tear its flesh with their strong cone-shaped teeth. Then they swallow the chunks of meat. When feeding on seals and other smaller prey, they just gulp them down whole.

Killer whales cruise through all the world's oceans and are often seen in the coastal waters of the northern Pacific. They may grow to be 30 feet (9 m) long and may weigh 20,000 pounds (9,072 kg).

In a killer whale herd, which is made up of several pods, these animals are extremely protective of one another. The animals help sick or injured members of the herd and also protect the young.

While the killer whale may be the fiercest toothed whale, the sperm whale is the largest. A male, when grown, averages 50 feet (15 m) in length—nearly as long as two killer whales end to end. The huge head, with its enormous jaws and teeth, makes up a third of the length. The sperm whale's teeth grow only in its lower jaw. The upper jaw has sockets into which the bottom teeth fit.

Except for the coldest polar regions, sperm whales live all over the world. They feed on many kinds of fish, but their favorite food is the giant squid. This huge octopuslike creature has tentacles that may stretch as long as the sperm whale itself.

To capture the giant squid, which lives in the deepest parts of the ocean, the sperm whale dives a mile or more! While diving, this whale can hold its breath for more than an hour.

During the 1700s and 1800s, whalers killed thousands of sperm whales. The "great white whale" in Herman Melville's novel, *Moby Dick or the White Whale*, was a sperm whale.

People hunted these animals for three substances important at that time: oil from the blubber, used in oil lamps; spermaceti (spur-muh-SEET-ee) from the head, used in candle making; and ambergris (AM-buhr-gris) sometimes found in the intestines, used in making perfume.

Sailors prized the sperm whale's teeth, which

■ *Passengers watch a sperm whale swim beside a ship off the coast of Mexico. This giant of the sea is exhaling a cloud of mist through the blowhole. Because of its huge head, this whale is one of the easiest to identify at sea. The average length of male sperm whales, the largest of all the toothed whales, is 50 feet (15 m).*

may grow up to 6 inches (15 cm) long. During voyages that might last for years, sailors worked designs into the teeth, an art called scrimshaw (SKRIM-shaw). Today, whaling is dying out. It is prohibited by the United States and many other countries. Electric lights have replaced oil lamps, and chemicals are used instead of spermaceti and ambergris.

All of the more than 60 other kinds of toothed whales are smaller than the sperm whale. To each species, biologists have assigned a scientific name. They classify some of the smaller ones as dolphins and some as porpoises. Dolphins usually have cone-shaped teeth and pointed, beaklike snouts. Porpoises generally are smaller than dolphins and usually have spade-shaped teeth and blunt noses. Many people, however, call all the smaller whales porpoises because there is also a *fish* called a dolphin.

Like other kinds of toothed whales, most dolphins and porpoises are social animals. Although some travel alone, nearly all seem to like to be with others of their kind. They often swim and hunt in herds made up of several pods. In such a large group, thousands of animals may swim together. Sailors

■ *Common dolphins leap in the Pacific off the coast of Mexico. Often traveling in herds of hundreds or even thousands, dolphins cooperate in food gathering and in caring for the young. While some group members carry out these tasks, others patrol the boundaries of the herd.*

often report seeing dolphins over many square miles of ocean surface.

Dolphins become very active when tracking schools of fish. They may leap out of the water and slap their bodies down hard. This frightens the fish and causes them to move closer together. Some of the dolphins circle their prey, while other dolphins dive in and eat. Then the circlers and the feeders may trade places.

Although dolphins and other toothed whales are air-breathing mammals, they can glide through the water as swiftly and easily as fish. Dolphins reach speeds of 30 miles (48 km) an hour. Their bodies are well suited to life in the sea.

In fact, a dolphin's body looks something like a submarine. Some designers of submarines and torpedoes have studied the bodies of dolphins to find ways of improving their own designs. The smooth, sleek shape of the dolphin helps it slide easily through the water. A large fin on its back, called a dorsal fin, helps the animal keep its balance. Front flippers help it steer and brake. A powerful tail is

■ *In the South Pacific Ocean, off the coast of New Zealand's South Island, a dusky dolphin leaps. Once it begins to leap, a dusky dolphin may make 40 to 50 jumps. The power for these graceful leaps comes from the movement of the dolphin's muscular tail. At the end—on the sides—are two lobes, called flukes.*

BILL CURTSINGER

■ *A beluga pokes its head above water (left). Unlike some other whales that range throughout the world's oceans, belugas live primarily in arctic waters. The name comes from the Russian word* belukha, *meaning "white."*

■ *Three male narwhals compete for females in cold Canadian waters (right). Two have crossed their corkscrew-shaped tusks in combat. These tusks earned the narwhal the nickname "unicorn of the sea."*

the dolphin's built-in propeller. While swimming, a dolphin moves its tail fins, called flukes, up and down. This motion differs from that of a fish's tail. If you watch a fish swimming, you will see that its tail moves from side to side. Both groups of animals move through the water equally well.

Dolphins and other toothed whales breathe through a nostril, called a blowhole, on the top of the head. Before diving, a whale inhales, then its blowhole closes tightly to keep the water out. When the animal resurfaces to exhale, the warm "blow" from its lungs hits the cooler air and forms a cloud of mist.

To find their way underwater and to locate prey, most toothed whales depend on echolocation (ek-oh-low-KAY-shun), a process for locating objects by using sound waves. (See pages 42–43.)

Toothed whales make many sounds, not from their mouths, but from air cavities beneath their blowholes. These sounds include whistles, squeals,

barks, and groans. Scientists think that dolphins may communicate information about their feelings, their identities, or the location of food.

The beluga (buh-LOO-guh), sometimes called the white whale, is one of the noisiest of all whales. This small, gentle creature, about 14 feet (4 m) long, was nicknamed the "sea canary" by early sailors. They could hear its high trilling chirps, squeaks, and clicks through the wooden hulls of their ships.

The beluga spends all its life mainly in the cold waters of the arctic region. It eats octopus, shrimp, and small fish. Beluga calves are born gray or brown. Gradually they turn white, becoming pure white by the time they are six or seven years old. Their whiteness helps the adults blend with the ice as they hunt. It also makes it easier for them to hide from enemies.

A close relative of the beluga is the narwhal, also an arctic creature. The narwhal is famous for its single long tooth—a twisted tusk of ivory. The

tusk usually grows only on male animals, and it grows from the upper jaw. No one is sure what the tusk is used for; however, it does help people identify male narwhals. Scientists believe the males use their tusks as weapons for fighting in order to win mates.

Long ago, explorers who found the tusks of dead narwhals believed they were the horns of unicorns, imaginary horselike beasts. The tusks were thought to have magical powers. Monarchs, including Queen Elizabeth I, of England, prized them. Some were worth the equivalent of thousands of dollars today.

The narwhal and most other toothed whales live in salty ocean waters. However, some toothed whales, called river dolphins, live in the fresh waters of rivers and lakes.

The boutu (BOH-too), or Amazon River dolphin, swims in the Amazon and the Orinoco Rivers, which flow through northern South America. The boutu grows to be about 8 feet (2 m) long. Although this dolphin can see fairly well, it depends mostly on echolocation to find food. Some of the tribal peoples of Brazil believe that killing a boutu brings bad luck.

Other kinds of dolphins live in rivers in India and in Pakistan. They are called susus (SOO-SOOZ). Practically blind, susus echolocate to find fish and shellfish in muddy water. Long snouts help them catch the prey.

■ *In South America, the boutu, called the Amazon River dolphin, moves slowly and feeds on fish and shellfish. Its eyes are of little use in the cloudy waters of the Amazon and Orinoco Rivers. To feel for crabs on the muddy river bottoms, the boutu uses the small bristles on its snout.*

The Chinese river dolphin lives in the Yangtze (YANG-SEE) River and in Lake Tung-t'ing. This dolphin, too, is nearly blind. According to legendary stories in China, the Chinese river dolphin is the ghost of a princess who drowned in Lake Tung-t'ing long ago.

Toothed whales come in different sizes, shapes, and colors. Nevertheless, all of them are mammals. As such, they share certain characteristics. For example, the females give birth to live young and feed them with milk from their own bodies.

A whale is born underwater, able to see and to swim well. Usually, the first thing it does is swim to the surface to breathe. If it does not, the mother or another adult female may push it up for a gulp of air.

Often, the mother dolphin has a helper, called an "aunt." She sometimes assists by swimming with the newborn calf while the mother rests.

After breathing, the calf must learn to drink its mother's milk. Usually within half an hour after birth, it seeks one of its mother's two nipples, which are located on her underside near her tail. Dolphins have solid, beaklike snouts, and the lips are not flexible. As a result, a young dolphin's way of nursing is unlike that of most mammals. It wraps its tongue around a nipple. Then the mother tightens muscles over her milk glands and squirts milk into its mouth. The calf gets a big drink in a hurry. In between squirts, it rises to the surface to breathe. It feeds about every 20 minutes.

A dolphin mother may nurse her young for a year and a half or more. The milk of a mother dolphin is very rich in protein and fat—so rich the calf doubles its birth weight in just two months.

Between the ages of five and fifteen months, the young also begins to eat its first solid food. As the calf grows, it stays close to its mother and other members of the pod.

Scientists studying the fossil history of whales believe that the ancestors of whales probably were land animals. Because the fossil record is not

■ *Near Hawaii, a spotted dolphin calf tags after its mother (left). They will stay together for at least a year.*

■ *Scientists studying the fossil history of dolphins believe that dolphin ancestors lived on land millions of years ago. (See the painting below.) Over time, their bodies became cylinder-shaped and nearly hairless. Their hind legs gradually disappeared, and the front legs became flippers. Their skulls shifted so that nostrils moved to the tops of the heads. Many species developed dorsal fins.*

complete, scientists are not certain what those ancestors might have looked like. The fossils indicate, however, that ungulates (UNG-gyuh-luts)—animals with hooves—share a common ancestry with dolphins and other whales. Over millions of years, some ungulates probably adapted to life in the sea.

Today, scientists are learning more about the senses of dolphins. These animals seem to have little or no sense of smell, but they probably have some sense of taste. Dolphins observed in captivity seem to prefer certain foods.

Touch is an important sense shared by all dolphins and whales. Their skin is smooth—like an inner tube—and sensitive. Members of family groups often touch and rub against each other. Mothers, especially, touch and stroke their young.

The eyesight of most toothed whales is fairly good both in and out of the water. We know, for example, that captive dolphins see well enough to catch balls and to touch targets high above

DAVID DOUBILET

■ *Heads above water, dolphins make sounds through air cavities beneath their blowholes. These animals have no vocal cords. Underwater, dolphins use sound to communicate, to find prey, and to avoid obstacles.*

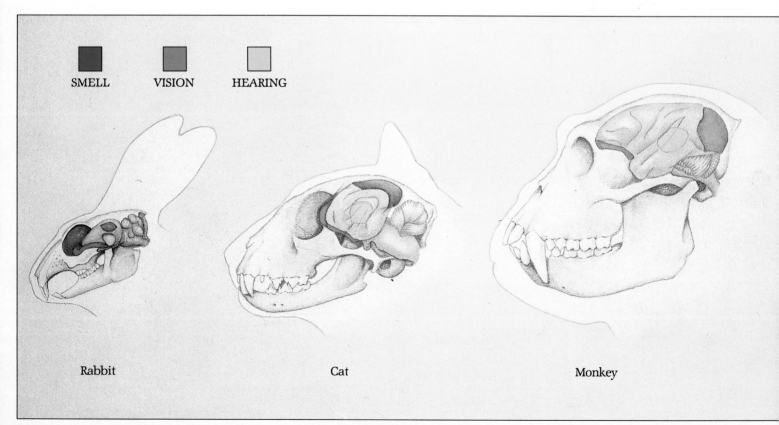

SMELL   VISION   HEARING

Rabbit   Cat   Monkey the water's surface. Seeing, however, is far less important to these animals than hearing.

In whales, hearing is the most highly developed sense. It helps them communicate, navigate, and find food in the ocean. They use a system of sound waves called echolocation. The dolphin's brain (see art below) shows the greatest development in the areas devoted to hearing.

To echolocate, dolphins send out high-pitched clicking sounds—as many as 1,200 a second. The clicks may be seven to eight times higher than sounds humans can hear. Scientists believe that dolphins make these sounds from air cavities beneath their blowholes. Then the sounds travel to the melon, a fatty organ on the forehead. The melon focuses the sounds and sends them forward in a pattern resembling the broad beam of a flashlight.

As a dolphin swims through the water, it moves its head back and forth to scan for objects ahead. When the clicking sounds hit an object, such as a rock or a fish, the sounds bounce back as echoes. Scientists believe that these echoes travel through the dolphin's lower jaw to the inner ear. Then they are transmitted to the brain. Much like a computer, the brain analyzes the echoes and tells the dolphin the location, size, and shape of the object. In experiments designed to test the dolphin's ability to echolocate, scientists have found that a blindfolded

■ *The painting below shows the brains of a rabbit, a cat, a monkey, and a dolphin. Different colors mark the areas devoted to smell, hearing, and vision. The dolphin has the keenest sense of hearing. It uses this sense in dark ocean depths to communicate, find food, and avoid obstacles. The dolphin sends out clicks from cavities in its head. When the sound hits an object, echoes travel to the dolphin, telling it the size, shape, and location of the object. On land, in a world of light and air, other animals rely more on smell and vision to find their way.*

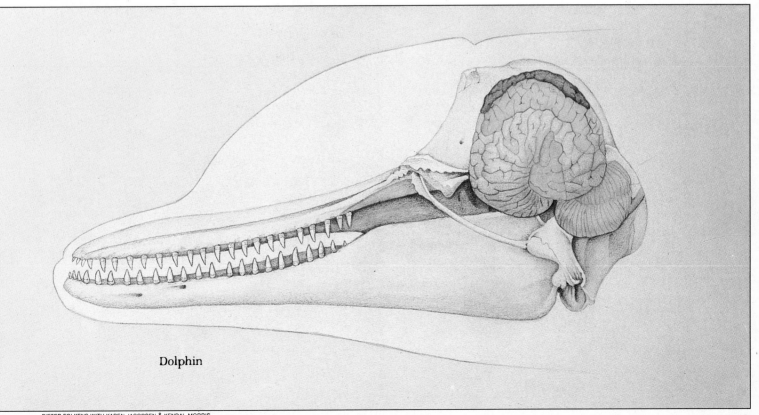

Dolphin

dolphin can tell the difference between a dime and a nickel when both are thrown into the dolphin's pool!

Scientists are also learning many things about the group life of toothed whales. In some groups, females may be the leaders. They are often old females, called "grandmothers."

Members of a herd help protect each other from sharks. For example, sharks often try to kill young dolphins. When a shark comes near, adult dolphins attack it from both sides. Using their hard snouts as weapons, they slam into the shark's soft sides. If they crush its gills, the shark can no longer obtain oxygen from the water, and it will die.

If any member of a dolphin group is hurt or sick, it sends out cries of distress. The other group members rush to help it. Observers in the wild have often seen groups of dolphins swim up under an injured animal to push it to the surface to breathe.

From ancient to modern times, there have been many stories of dolphins giving this same kind of help to humans. Some scientists think that these animals naturally push sinking objects up to the water's surface. This behavior may account for their sometimes helping people in distress.

On the next pages, read an ancient story about how a young musician befriended dolphins and how they later rescued him from drowning.

■ *Spotted dolphins swim near the Bahamas. Social animals, dolphins help each other in many ways. While some circle a school of fish, others eat them. Then the dolphins may change places. If one is sick or injured, others may support it and push it to the surface to breathe. Dolphins even nap together at the surface.*

HOWARD HALL

Arion and the Dolphins

Long ago, according to an ancient Greek legend, there lived a young man named Arion (uh-RYE-uhn). He loved to sing and to play the lyre, a small stringed instrument. He also loved dolphins and would play for them.

Arion lived in the palace of a king in the Greek city of Corinth. He learned of a musical contest in Sicily, a Mediterranean island south of Italy. First prize was all the gold the winner could carry. Arion decided to enter the contest, and he set sail for Sicily.

During the journey, he practiced singing and playing his lyre every day. Dolphins swam beside the ship because they loved his music.

In Sicily, Arion played and sang for a big crowd at the contest. He easily won first prize. After gathering all the gold he could carry, he returned to the ship to sail for home.

On the voyage back, the sailors decided to kill him and take his gold. When they ordered him to jump overboard, he made one request: to sing a final song. After singing, he hurled himself into the sea, still holding his lyre.

As Arion plunged under the waves, he suddenly felt himself being lifted up. His old friends, attracted by his music, had come to rescue him. A dolphin carried Arion home on its back, faster than the ship could sail.

When Arion reached the palace, he told the king of the sailors' deed. Furious, the king waited for the men to return. Then he asked them where Arion was. "He stayed behind in Sicily," they lied. When Arion stepped before them, they were terrified and begged the king for mercy. Instead, he threatened them with punishment. At that, the sailors ran away, leaving Arion's gold behind.

Immediately, Arion ran down to the seashore to thank the dolphins. He played for them, and they leapt joyfully in the waves.

FEDERICO CASTELLUCCIO

CHAPTER 3

GETTING TO KNOW THE WHALES

Curious killer whales spy hop near the western coast of Canada. Biologist John Ford observes them from a boat close by.

49

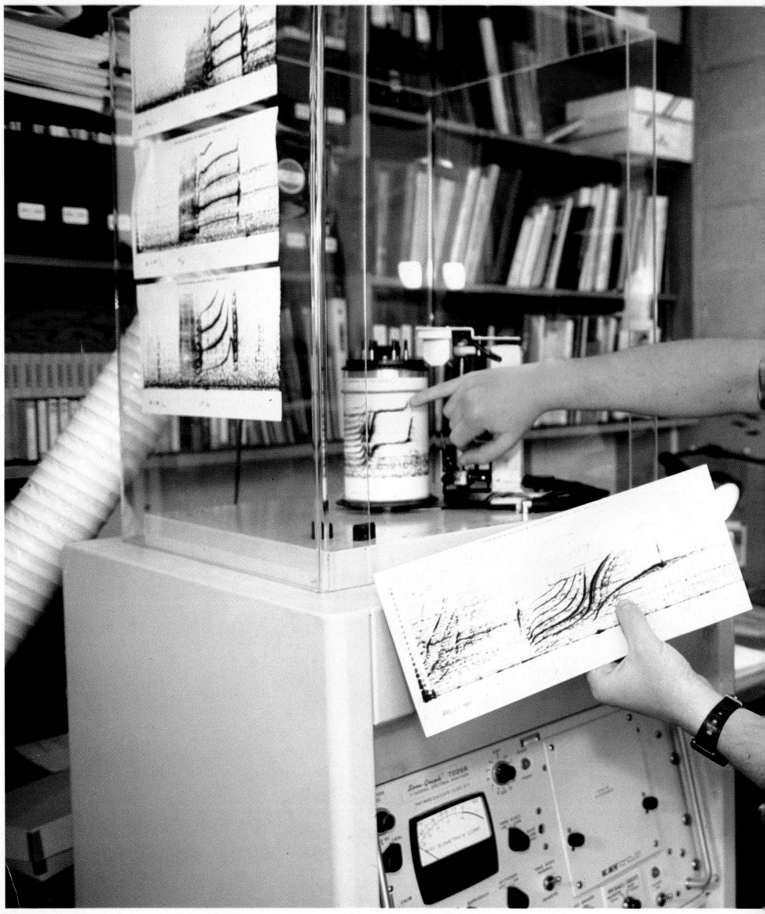

■ Using a special machine, Dr. John Ford makes visual charts of the calls of wild killer whales. He recorded their calls off the coast of British Columbia, a province of Canada. "By studying these charts," says Dr. Ford, "we have learned that each pod of killer whales has its own 'dialect,' or special pattern, of calls." Dr. Ford believes that members of a pod can identify each other by recognizing their common dialect, even over long distances. Today, scientists studying toothed whales are beginning to understand many of the mysteries of these animals.

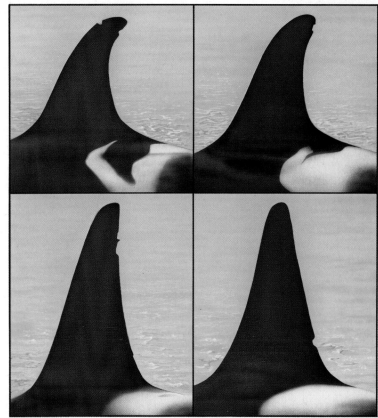

■ *Photographs of killer whale dorsal fins help Dr. Michael Bigg (left) identify individual animals. A microscope reveals small details in the pictures. As Dr. Bigg spots the same whales in different places, he can keep track of their movements.*

■ *Like a human face, each killer whale fin is one of a kind (right). Fins of females, above, are usually curved. Fins of adult males, below, are straight. Scars, as well as the white patches near the fins, are also different on each whale. Such details help scientists identify individuals.*

What is it like to study wild sea animals? In many ways, it's a lot like being a private detective! Scientists spend hours quietly tracking and watching dolphins and other whales. Researchers even eavesdrop on the underwater "conversations" of whales and take photographs to help keep track of them. In the process, scientists get to know the animals, learn their secrets, and sometimes meet them face to face.

Dr. Michael Bigg is a scientist who works for the Canadian government. He helps the government protect the killer whales that live along the coast of British Columbia, a province in western Canada. Each year, Dr. Bigg takes a killer whale census, or population count. He does this by going out in a small boat and photographing the whales. At the same time, he makes notes about their activities. Since 1973, he has kept photographs of the dorsal fin of every killer whale in the entire area.

"Each animal's dorsal fin is different," says Dr. Bigg. "I discovered that photographing these fins was an excellent way to identify the animals. By comparing each year's new photographs with those I have in a master file of known whales, I can tell which whales I've spotted."

What can Dr. Bigg learn from his census information? "We can tell where the whales travel, which pods they belong to, and a lot about their family histories and lifespans." Dr. Bigg thinks that males may live 50 years and that females may live 75.

Other scientists have used Dr. Bigg's identification system to study British Columbia's killer whales. One of these experts is Alexandra Morton, an American researcher in animal behavior.

Mrs. Morton carefully observes the identified whales' activities and behaviors year-round. She notes when they feed, play, and travel. At the same time, she records the sounds of the whales, using

53

■ *Near the coast of British Columbia, researcher Alexandra Morton (left) takes notes on the activities of killer whales with a computer. At the same time, a device under the water records their calls. By matching the computer notes with the recording, she learns which calls go with which behaviors.*

■ *Listening to the sounds of Commerson's dolphins, Dr. Frank Awbrey (right), at Sea World in San Diego, holds a chart of the recorded calls.*

underwater microphones. Her goal is to learn what the killer whales communicate during their activities. "Their 'language' is completely different from ours," she says. So far, Mrs. Morton has noted that killer whales make 62 different types of sounds. She has recorded the number of times each sound is used during various activities. The whales make the same sounds while in different emotional states, such as calmness or excitement. However, the number of times each sound is made varies. According to Mrs. Morton, it will take years of work to learn more.

Do the whales pay attention to the scientists who study them? Mrs. Morton believes they do. She remembers one experience in particular.

One afternoon, she was studying the killer whales in a small boat. She was so busy she didn't notice that a heavy fog had drifted in and settled over her. Suddenly, on her underwater microphones, she heard the booming roar of a giant luxury liner

coming right toward her! She realized she was in a narrow pass between two islands. Without a compass, she could not tell how to head toward shore and get out of the ship's path.

Just then, she remembers, killer whales popped up all around her. Instead of swimming quickly away, they began to swim slowly just ahead of her boat, as she followed. Soon, she reached the edge of the fog and saw land. Then the whales left her. Although the story sounds incredible, she believes the whales may have saved her life that day.

Dr. Frank Awbrey, a biologist at San Diego State University, specializes in echolocation sounds of toothed whales. "Most toothed whales, such as killer whales, make clicking sounds to echolocate," says Dr. Awbrey. "But not all," he continues. "Commerson's dolphins and Dall's porpoises make a different kind of high-pitched sound. It is similar to the sonar of some bats." Dr. Awbrey thinks this may be an

adaptation to help these animals find food in their particular environments.

Canadian biologists Dr. John and Deborah Ford study killer whales off Canada's coasts. They study narwhals in arctic waters, as well.

"Narwhals are very different, socially, from killer whales," says Dr. Ford. "They do not seem to form pods as killer whales do. But numbers of male narwhals often congregate. They use their tusks to fight for females." Many of the males have scars on their heads from such contests. Older males have the longest tusks and probably win the most matches.

Although the Fords studied narwhals in a fragile kayak, they never worried about being attacked. "The animals were very curious," says Dr. Ford. "One female we saw was fascinated by our boat. Every time we dipped our paddles into the water, she swam right up under the kayak. We had to paddle back to shore to keep her from tipping us over."

Early whale-watchers may have had experiences similar to the Fords'. On the next page, you'll find a fanciful tale of the Middle Ages that probably grew out of such an encounter.

If scientists discover (Continued on page 61)

■ *Drifting quietly in a kayak, biologists John and Deborah Ford observe male narwhals and photograph them near Baffin Island, Canada. For generations, Canadian Eskimos, called Inuit, have hunted narwhals, using kayaks to approach them quietly. The Fords have observed that the males use their tusks to battle for mates, much as male deer use antlers. The ivory tusks grow up to 10 feet (3 m) long.*

St. Brendan, Ancient Whale-Watcher

Long before scientists observed whales in the wild, early sailors on their voyages noticed these amazing creatures. One of the earliest whale-watchers may have been an Irishman named Brendan.

Brendan was a Christian monk who lived about A.D. 500. He went on long voyages to tell people about his religion. Brendan and his crew of monks sailed in a boat called a curragh (KUH-ruhk). It was made of leather hides stretched over a wooden frame, and it was equipped with sails. On one such journey, Brendan kept a diary. In it, he told of natural wonders seen along the way, including icebergs, volcanoes, and spouting whales.

Over the years, many people added their own ideas to Brendan's diary. During the Middle Ages, this mixture of fact and fiction became a popular legend. Because his descriptions of whales are very detailed, however, researchers believe that Brendan actually saw these animals.

Part of Brendan's story tells of his meeting a large sperm whale. He called the whale Jasconius (Jass-CONE-ee-us). The name comes from an old Irish word for "fish," with a Latin ending.

In the story, Brendan and his crew anchored their boat near what they thought was a treeless island. Unknown to them, the "island" was really Jasconius, fast asleep! The monks made camp on Jasconius's back, built a campfire, and prepared to cook a meal. Just as their pot began to boil, the monks felt the "ground" start to tremble and move. It was Jasconius, waking up!

The monks fled in terror back to their boat. Then, as they watched in amazement, Jasconius slowly swam away—with the fire still burning on his back.

58

FEDERICO CASTELLUCCIO

■ *At a research camp near the Seal River, in Manitoba, scientists prepare belugas for tagging (left). Trevor Friesen positions one beluga as David St. Aubin waits to place small plastic tags in the whales' blubber.*

■ *Working gently, Dr. Joseph Geraci (right) takes blood from a beluga. Susan Waters assists. Blood tests show how the whales react to tags under the skin. Later, brightly colored streamers attached to the tags will be easy to see from aircraft.*

NATIONAL GEOGRAPHIC PHOTOGRAPHER BATES LITTLEHALES (BOTH)

(*Continued from page 57*) where whales go in different seasons, it will be easier to understand our friends of the sea and to protect them. For these reasons, the governments of several countries are trying to track the movements of whales.

The Canadian government asked scientists from the University of Guelph (GWELF), in the province of Ontario, to test new materials for tagging belugas. These materials had to be harmless to the animals, yet long-lasting and clearly visible.

In 1984 and in 1985, University of Guelph scientists, headed by Dr. Joseph Geraci, set up summer camps near the Seal River, in northern Manitoba, a province of Canada. To test various kinds of tagging materials, they captured several belugas. Then they inserted small, thin pins of different kinds of plastic into the whales' blubber. "We believe this operation was harmless to the whales. It seemed to cause them little discomfort," says David St. Aubin, a specialist who studied the whales' skin growth and reaction to the pins. "We found that the best tagging material was a plastic that surgeons use to replace human tissue in operations," he adds. "This plastic stays in the animals' blubber but does not cause infections. The skin heals rapidly over it."

Before releasing the whales, the scientists attached brightly colored streamers to the tags they had inserted. The streamers will be easily visible to experts who fly over the arctic area. They will keep watch on the whales' movements in the coming years. Scientists want to know how faithfully the belugas return to the same places and how much visiting among groups takes place.

Dr. Randall Wells, of the University of California at Santa Cruz, is another scientist who studies whales. For 17 years, he has been observing the family relationships within a community of Atlantic bottlenose dolphins. (*Continued on page 64*)

■ *Researchers with a net encircle wild bottlenose dolphins near Sarasota, Florida (left). They measure each animal, take a blood sample, then let the dolphin go. The first time a dolphin is studied, one of its teeth is removed. The animal's age can be discovered by observing a section of the tooth under a microscope. Dr. Randall Wells (below) has headed this research project for 17 years. "By studying the same dolphins over three generations," he says, "we have learned about their family structure and social behavior."*

(Continued from page 61)　　　These dolphins live in coastal waters near Sarasota, Florida.

Each year, Dr. Wells and other scientists observe the same dolphins. Helping in the study are volunteers from EARTHWATCH, an organization that supports many kinds of research. Dr. Wells and his group spend hours following the dolphins and photographing them from small boats. Then they capture the animals in shallow water to examine them and to take blood samples.

"By studying the dolphins' blood, we can learn which animals are related to which," says Dr. Wells. "We have been observing a hundred or so animals that live together on a permanent basis. We can now recognize as many as three generations, and we want to learn more about relationships among

■ *Scars show where a shark has attacked a dolphin (right). Examination of the tooth spacing and the scar shape may tell researchers the species of shark. "About 16 percent of dolphins have shark-bite scars," says Dr. Wells.*

■ *Researchers Suzanne Ganley and Rick Spaulding (below) record a dolphin's call using a suction-cup microphone. Working as assistants to Dr. Peter Tyack, they hope to find out how dolphins learn their calls and how they use them to "talk" to each other.*

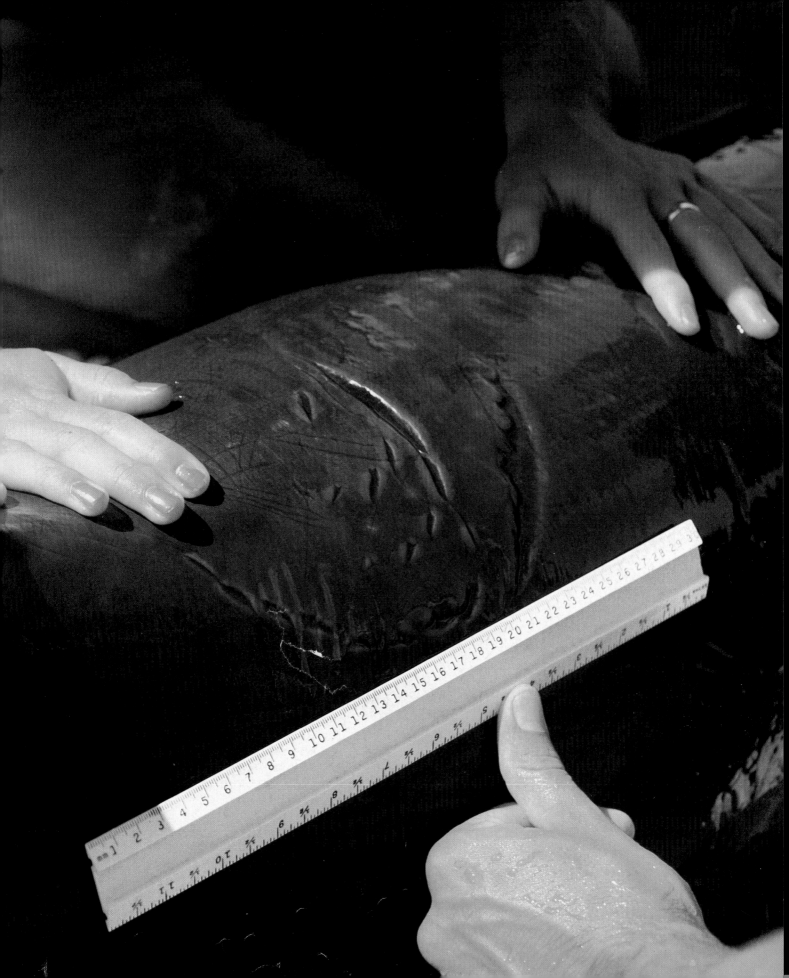

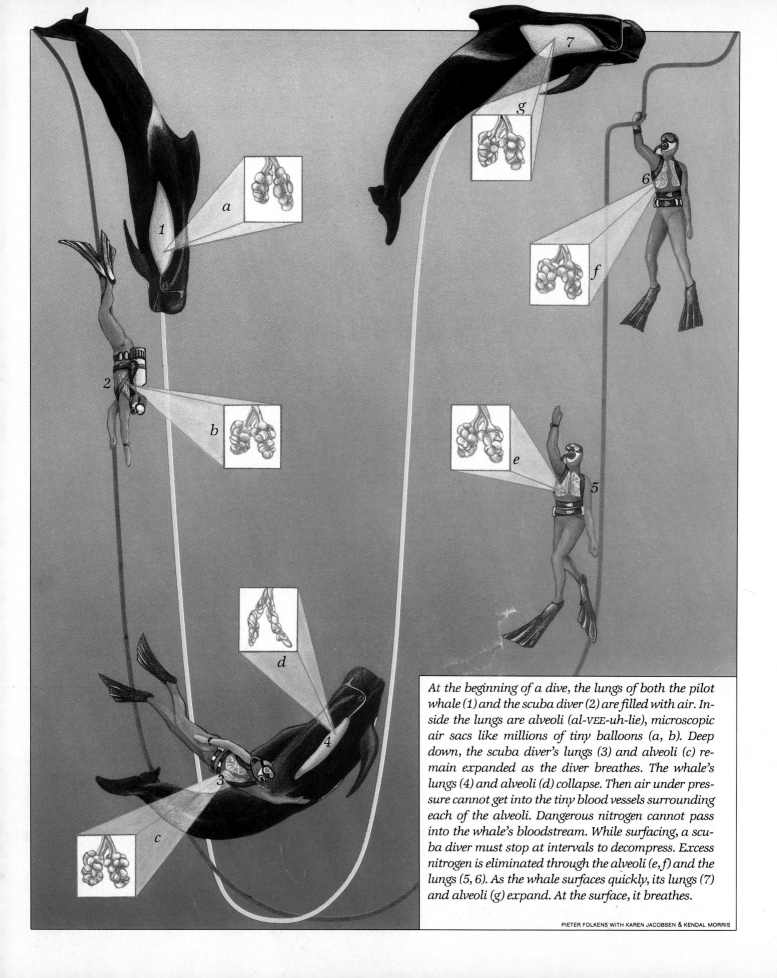

At the beginning of a dive, the lungs of both the pilot whale (1) and the scuba diver (2) are filled with air. Inside the lungs are alveoli (al-VEE-uh-lie), microscopic air sacs like millions of tiny balloons (a, b). Deep down, the scuba diver's lungs (3) and alveoli (c) remain expanded as the diver breathes. The whale's lungs (4) and alveoli (d) collapse. Then air under pressure cannot get into the tiny blood vessels surrounding each of the alveoli. Dangerous nitrogen cannot pass into the whale's bloodstream. While surfacing, a scuba diver must stop at intervals to decompress. Excess nitrogen is eliminated through the alveoli (e, f) and the lungs (5, 6). As the whale surfaces quickly, its lungs (7) and alveoli (g) expand. At the surface, it breathes.

■ *The painting (left) compares the body of a scuba diver with that of a pilot whale as they dive deep, then return to the surface. When scuba divers surface too quickly, they may get the bends, a painful and sometimes fatal condition. The problem starts when nitrogen—a gas in the air we breathe—dissolves in a scuba diver's bloodstream under the heavy pressure of deep water. A quick return to the surface makes the dissolved nitrogen change back into a gas. Nitrogen bubbles in the body cause severe pain in the joints and tissues—the bends. In contrast, a whale can surface quickly. When it dives, its flexible rib cage collapses under pressure, compressing the lungs. This keeps nitrogen from getting into the whale's bloodstream. The whale's lungs expand to their normal size as the animal rises quickly to the surface.*

fathers, mothers, and calves within the community."

As Dr. Wells examines the dolphins in the water, they may examine *him* with the sounds they make. "It feels like tickling, usually in my chest," he says.

For years, the U. S. Navy has studied and tested dolphins. The Navy wanted to learn, among other things, how dolphins and other whales can dive deep and return quickly to the surface without getting the bends. The bends are painful and sometimes fatal.

■ *How deep can dolphins dive? A Pacific bottlenose dolphin named Lii (LEE-EE) helps the U. S. Navy find out (below). As a buzzer is lowered from a boat, Lii dives to push it, finally reaching 1,760 feet (536 m).*

Scuba divers can get the bends if they surface too quickly. The bends are caused by nitrogen bubbles in the body.

Dr. Samuel Ridgway explains how dolphins and other whales avoid this condition. He is a research veterinarian who has helped train dolphins for the U. S. Naval Ocean Systems Center, in San Diego, California. "The dolphin's secret," Dr. Ridgway says, "is a flexible rib cage. When a whale dives, its rib cage and lungs collapse under the pressure of deep water. This keeps any air from passing between the lungs and the rest of the body. As a result, nitrogen cannot dissolve in the bloodstream, change into bubbles, and cause the bends when the whale surfaces."

Other mysteries remain to be solved. For example, how do dolphins "talk" to each other? Do they have a language? Could they understand *our* language, and could we talk to them? Dr. Louis Herman is one of the scientists searching for answers.

A psychology professor at the University of Hawaii, Dr. Herman tutors two female Atlantic bottlenose dolphins in a language program. One dolphin is called Phoenix, the name of a legendary bird that was reborn from its own ashes. The other is called Akeakamai, which means "lover of wisdom" in Hawaiian. Dr. Herman wants to learn if dolphins can understand combinations of words in sentences.

He has taught the two dolphins vocabularies of 35 to 40 "words" for such English words as "ball," "hoop," "Frisbee," "right," "left," "touch," and "fetch." Phoenix has learned a "language" of sounds. An underwater computer makes the sounds for her. Akeakamai has learned a language of visual signs made by people using their arms and hands. Each

■ *At a trainer's signal, Phoenix (FEE-nix) and Akeakamai (uh-KAY-yuh-kuh-MY) leap together (right). These two Atlantic bottlenose dolphins spend two sessions a day learning "language skills." Their tutor is Dr. Louis Herman (below), of the University of Hawaii.*

■ *Time off from school! Dr. Herman swims with Phoenix in a weekend play session (below). Such play periods help strengthen bonds between the dolphin students and their tutors. Playing also helps the animals relax.*

of the two languages has different rules about how words go together. The different word orders are designed to challenge the dolphins' ability to understand sentences. For example, a tutor might say to Phoenix, "Ball fetch hoop." This means, "Carry the ball to the hoop." The same command to Akeakamai would be given as "hoop—ball—fetch." The dolphins in this research project have been given sentences of up to five words—in many combinations.

"Surprisingly," says Dr. Herman, "we have found that both of the dolphins understand sentences and respond to them equally well." Does Dr. Herman think humans may be able to carry on conversations with dolphins one day? "That's a long way off," he says. "What we're doing is like teaching a child to read. It's just the first step. Animals that can learn the basics of language have great possibilities."

■ *Arms in a circle, Beth Seymour signals "ball" to Akeakamai (left). Beth will use other hand and arm signals to form the sentence, "Touch the ball at left." Akeakamai follows instructions. Beth wears goggles to keep the dolphin from seeing the direction of her gaze.*

■ *Phoenix (below) understands a language of computer sounds. Here, she responds to the sentence, "Take the 'hoop' at the surface to the 'hoop' at the pool bottom."*

CHAPTER 4

HELPING OUR FRIENDS OF THE SEA

Dr. Jay Sweeney listens to the lungs of Misty, a bottlenose dolphin, at Marineland in Los Angeles, California.

■ *Working quickly but gently, dolphin handlers remove a bottlenose dolphin from a net. Next, they will lift the animal into a boat. They are taking this dolphin for an oceanarium. The men must handle the dolphin carefully to avoid hurting its delicate skin. To collect a wild dolphin, a sea park has to obtain a special permit from the U. S. government. Park officials then work with licensed collectors, usually veterinarians, who continually check the animals' health. In the wild, dolphins, like all marine mammals, are protected by U. S. law. In captivity, people give them expert care.*

■ *After collecting three dolphins off the coast of Florida, Pam Barzette and Tom Hopkins pour water over the animals (left). The dolphins are wrapped in sheets so they will stay moist and cool. They will go to the EPCOT Center's Living Seas, in Orlando.*

■ *Cradling a dolphin before it is lifted into a boat, Dr. Jay Sweeney checks it over (right). "This dolphin, later named Christie, was calm," he says. "Nervous animals don't do well in captivity."*

HENNING CHRISTOPH (BOTH)

Dr. Jay Sweeney is a special kind of veterinarian. He takes care of marine mammals, including dolphins and other toothed whales. One of Dr. Sweeney's most important jobs is to supervise the collecting of wild dolphins for sea parks and oceanariums. He is one of very few experts allowed by the U. S. government to do this.

On a warm day early in 1985, Dr. Sweeney and staff members from the EPCOT Center's Living Seas, in Orlando, Florida, set out to collect dolphins for a new sea-life exhibit. In a specially equipped boat, they went to an area off the Florida coast near Fort Myers. There, they spotted a group of bottlenose dolphins swimming in shallow water. Under Dr. Sweeney's supervision, they carefully placed a large net around the animals.

Once the dolphins were encircled by the net, the staff members and Dr. Sweeney got into the water. They looked for healthy adult animals. Under law,

no pregnant females or nursing calves may be collected. Each animal must be at least 6½ feet (2 m) long. After each dolphin was chosen, Dr. Sweeney went near it and gently stroked it and held it in his arms. "These animals respond well to touch and usually just relax in my arms," he says. "By holding a dolphin, I can tell if it is calm. If a dolphin seems very nervous and excited, it will not adjust well to captivity, and I do not allow it to be collected."

Next, the crew carefully lifted each dolphin with a stretcher and the side of the net into the boat. Staff members kept the dolphins moist and cool. Then they took the animals to a holding lagoon in the Florida Keys, a chain of islands off the southern tip of Florida. There, Dr. Sweeney examined each animal to make sure it was healthy. He watched as trainers worked with the animals, winning their trust and teaching them to accept food.

Finally, after becoming used to people, the

dolphins—two females and three males—were flown to their new home at EPCOT Center.

The five dolphins were named Christie, Katie, Bob, Toby, and Tyke. Although their new home—The Living Seas—is many miles from the ocean, it is remarkably like the ocean. The main exhibit is like a Caribbean coral reef. A doughnut-shaped tank, it is filled with nearly six million gallons of salt water and furnished with colorful corals. In the exhibit, 7,000 tropical fish, stingrays, well-fed sharks, and even sea turtles swim freely as visitors watch through viewing windows.

In addition, The Living Seas has a smaller research pool. There, visitors can watch as scientists study sea animals to learn about their behavior.

What's it like to swim with dolphins? Have you ever wondered? In writing this book, I was lucky enough to find out. Kym Murphy, corporate manager of marine technology at The Living Seas, invited me to visit the artificial coral reef exhibit and swim with the new dolphins there. For my adventure, I put on scuba gear and slipped into the huge coral reef environment, 27 feet (8 m) deep.

■ *On the move. Trainers from the EPCOT Center's Living Seas carry a dolphin from a lagoon to a truck. The truck will take the animal to an air-conditioned helicopter. While experts keep it comfortable, the dolphin will be flown to a new home in The Living Seas coral reef exhibit.*

■ *Safe arrival. After the trip by helicopter to* EPCOT *Center, a dolphin is lifted by a crane to the exhibit floor of The Living Seas. Minutes later, staff members helped it slide into a holding pool. Says Living Seas animal specialist Gretchen Jacobs: "The dolphins showed almost no distress from traveling. The trip was short—only four hours out of the water. The whirring of the helicopter seemed to relax the animals."*

It was like a dreamworld. Through the rippling water, I saw swaying sea plants and pink and yellow corals branching at my feet. Brilliantly colored fish darted everywhere. Then—straight ahead—I saw dolphins! They were the two females, Christie and Katie. Like graceful dancers, they twirled and glided side by side in an underwater ballet.

I swam near them and stretched out my hand. The dolphins looked at me curiously with their expressive brown eyes as if to ask, "Who are you?" Then they flicked their powerful tails and dashed out of my reach, only to circle around and sneak up behind me. Then they gently nuzzled me on my back! Before I could turn around, they zipped out of reach again. I soon realized they were playing a game of tag—and *I* was it!

For nearly an hour, the dolphins circled around me, enjoying this game. Their bodies, weighing more than 300 pounds (136 kg) each, felt extremely powerful as they whirled close to me. Yet I never for a moment felt any fear—only a sense of their shy friendliness and playful curiosity.

I was glad to know that these gentle creatures are well cared for in captivity. On page 83, you can read the story of Pelorus Jack, the first wild dolphin to be protected by a country. *(Continued on page 84)*

■ *From a balcony at* EPCOT *Center, visitors observe two new female dolphins, Christie and Katie. Large windows at eye level with the animals provide underwater views for other fans. One of the trainers is in the water behind the dolphins. In this research pool, experts are studying how dolphins echolocate, communicate, and sleep.*

WAYNE EASTEP

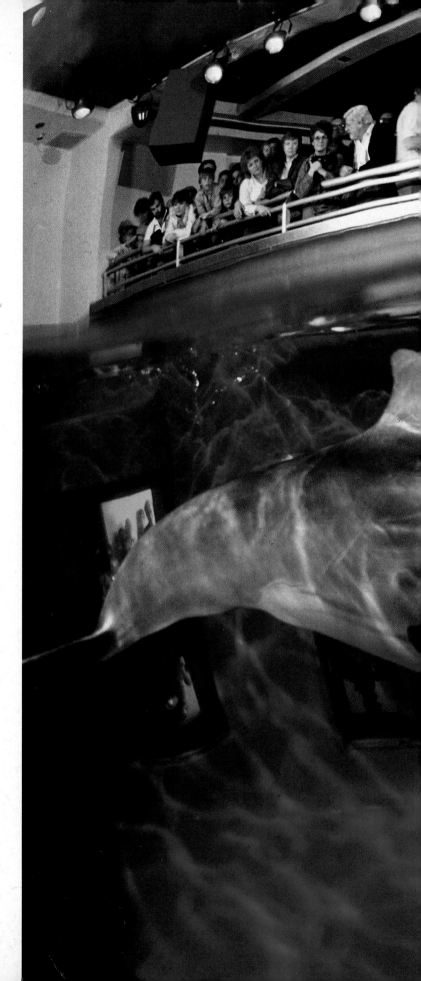

Pelorus Jack, Dolphin Escort

From 1888 to 1912, a dolphin delighted steamship passengers near Pelorus Sound, a stretch of ocean between the two main islands of New Zealand. He was a Risso's dolphin—heavyset and whitish gray—called Pelorus Jack by his fans. For 24 years, he regularly met large ships traveling near the pass.

As soon as Pelorus Jack heard the noise of a ship's engines, day or night, he would race through the water, overtake the steamer, then leap up to catch a free ride on its bow wave. For about six miles (10 km), he would ride the wave like a surfer.

Jack became so popular that tourists often made special trips from far away just to see him and to take his photograph. When they saw him coming, they would cry out, "Here comes Pelorus Jack!" One regular passenger wrote: " I would look up and see Pelorus Jack approaching at racing speed with great leaps out of the water, often ending close by with a mighty splash . . . ."

Jack apparently could swim faster than any of the ships could travel. He always chose the fastest ones. The faster the ship, the more exciting was Jack's ride.

In 1904, New Zealand made it illegal to kill or to capture any Risso's dolphin in the area. Pelorus Jack was the first dolphin ever to be legally protected.

Finally, after nearly a quarter century, Jack disappeared. People had many ideas about what had happened to their friend. Most experts believe, however, that Jack simply died of old age.

Why did Jack follow the ships for so many years? Why was he always alone? Some people think he may have been separated from his own kind as a calf. Perhaps he was seeking company. No one really knows for sure.

FEDERICO CASTELLUCCIO

83

(Continued from page 80) Today, many countries, including the United States, protect dolphins and other marine mammals with laws. The U. S. Marine Mammal Protection Act of 1972 states that no one may harm or disturb these animals in U. S. waters. Under this law, fishermen must release dolphins or porpoises caught in their nets.

For many years, U. S. tuna fishermen have relied on dolphins to help them find and catch the largest kinds of tuna. Yellowfin tuna, which may weigh more than 100 pounds (45 kg) each, often follow herds of dolphins. They usually accompany spotted or spinner dolphins, swimming under a herd. Scientists think the tuna may stay with the dolphins to feed on the same small fish the dolphins hunt.

In the 1950s, fishermen began using large nets called purse seines (SAYNZ) to catch tuna. These nets have made it possible to take many more tuna than could be caught using earlier methods. Purse seines can hold thousands of dolphins along with the fish. Many of the dolphins captured in this way died before the fishermen were able to release them.

R. A. ROWLETT

■ *On a salmon fishing boat, Japanese fishermen work to release two Dall's porpoises caught in a net. Some porpoises die from such entanglement. Working under an agreement with the U. S. government, Japanese fishermen are trying to reduce the number accidentally captured. One of their methods is to attach noise-making devices to their nets. The devices make pinging sounds that warn the porpoises to keep away.*

1

2

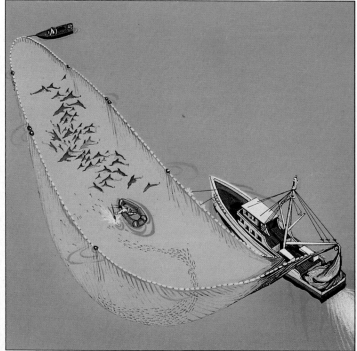

DOROTHY MICHELE NOVICK

Not wanting to kill the dolphins, leaders in the tuna industry invented a method of releasing these animals. It is called the "backdown" procedure. The art below shows how it works. Backdown is difficult, and it takes a lot of skill—but it saves the lives of thousands of dolphins each year.

Dominic Castagnola, from San Diego, California, is one of the tuna boat captains practicing this procedure. Dominic has been a tuna fisherman since his teenage years. His boat is called the *Antonina C.* Both Dominic's father and his grandfather were tuna boat captains.

"I've seen dolphins near our boats thousands of times," says Dominic. "First, they come up behind the boat, and then they swim alongside it. They like to leap and play in the big wave the front of the boat makes—the bow wave. I've seen them riding on the curl of this wave just the way human surfers do. The dolphins seem to love it! It's fun to watch them. They're wild and quick and free."

When it's time for business and the *Antonina C.* heads out to look for tuna, Dominic and his crew watch for herds of dolphins. They know that where there are dolphins, there are likely to be tuna.

When the crew spots the splashing of dolphins in the water, they signal their captain. Dominic climbs high up to the crow's nest at the top of the ship's mast. From there, he observes the dolphin herd. By radio, he orders a group of his men in

■ *Because tuna often swim with dolphins, tuna fishermen catch many dolphins in their nets. They use a special method to release the dolphins (below). 1) As the net is set, the main boat circles both dolphins and tuna. Speedboats keep the animals in a tight bunch. 2) When the net is closed, the captain begins to back the main boat away. The far end of the net, attached to a speedboat, will be pulled underwater. 3) A raftsman inside the net splashes water to herd the dolphins toward the end of the net. There they can escape, flushed out over a special fine-mesh panel. 4) Watching to make sure all dolphins escape, the men in the speedboat and raft reach into the water and hand-release the last few stragglers.*

3

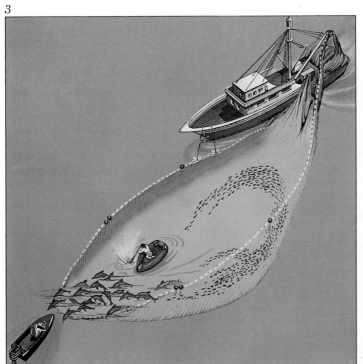

4

speedboats to follow and chase the dolphins. "The boat drivers are something like cowboys," says Dominic. "Imagine men on horses herding and corralling cattle. That's what the men in the speedboats do. They zigzag around the dolphins and herd them into a tight bunch."

Once the dolphins are in a close group, Dominic pilots the tuna boat in a circle around them, enclosing both the dolphins and the tuna inside a net. A machine then tightens and closes the net bottom. It works much like a drawstring bag.

Next, the important step of maneuvering the tuna boat to release the dolphins begins. "I put the boat in reverse and back away from the net," says Dominic. "This pulls the net in an oblong loop. The far end of the net dips underwater, and the dolphins slip over the top like water pouring out of a pitcher."

Crewmen in a speedboat and a raft may need to help the last few dolphins out of the net by hand. They make sure no tuna, which stay deeper in the net, escape. This hand-releasing of dolphins can be risky for several reasons, according to Dominic.

"You must be careful because dolphins are very

■ *Dolphins in a tuna net wait to go free. When the end of the net dips underwater, they will be swept out. One dolphin forces its way over the floats that hold the net. This end of the net is made of fine mesh so the dolphins' snouts will not catch in it.*

powerful animals," Dominic says. "You never grab dolphins by their tails. They could lash out and crush you with their tail flukes. Instead, you grab their snouts. Then you use your other arm to grab their dorsal fins, and you just help them over the net."

By far the biggest danger in hand-releasing dolphins, according to Dominic, is sharks. Large sharks are often trapped and hidden in the net with the other fish and the dolphins.

"Once," says Dominic, "while releasing dolphins, a crew member put his arm into the water, and a huge shark came out of nowhere and went straight for it. The man pulled his arm away, but the shark lunged out of the water and slashed the man's shoulder with its teeth. The shoulder had to have 70 stitches. He was lucky. He could have easily lost his arm or been pulled in by the shark and killed."

In spite of the danger, the tuna fishermen want to release the dolphins, says Dominic. They are proud that they can successfully release more than 90 percent of all the (Continued on page 92)

■ *Seen near the water's surface, dolphins appear to swim out over a net. Actually, they are being swept out by flowing water as the tuna boat pulls this end of the net beneath the surface. This is part of a procedure called "backdown," which enables tuna fishermen to release thousands of dolphins each year. Usually dolphins will not swim out of a net or jump over its edge on their own.*

WILLIAM L. HIGH

■ Rescuers guide a group of false killer whales out to sea (right). They had stranded, or beached, themselves. Although the whales were led to deeper water, they did not survive. Experts found they had worms in certain of their head cavities. The worms may have interfered with echolocation.

■ Anne Lacy, of Albany, New York, examines a stranded common dolphin (below). Strandings of individual animals may be caused by disease, old age, or injuries from sharks.

■ *Why do toothed whales mysteriously strand themselves? This painting shows some possible reasons. Worms in the heart (1), lungs (2), or brain (3) may make the animals sick and unable to swim or echolocate properly. Noise, like that caused by ships probing for oil (4), may injure, frighten, or confuse whales, causing them to become stranded. Whales may swim ashore to escape danger at sea, such as a killer whale attack (5). Some whales may get caught in certain kinds of fishing nets (6), drown, and later wash ashore. Whales may make errors in navigation, becoming stranded on sloping shores (7) before detecting land.*

DOROTHY MICHELE NOVICK

91

(Continued from page 87)   dolphins caught. "We risk our lives to save them," Dominic continues, "but it's worth it. Without the dolphins, our job would be a lot harder. We depend on them to help us find tuna."

Sometimes dolphins and other toothed whales need human help when they strand themselves. Why the animals become stranded, often in huge numbers, is still a mystery. (See pages 90–91 for a number of theories about causes.)

To help stranded animals, experts recommend several emergency measures:

1) Keep water from covering the animals' blowholes and getting into their lungs. It might cause them to drown.

2) Keep the animals' skin cool and moist. Their skin can easily crack and burn in the sun. Apply lanolin cream; then cover the skin with wet cloth.

3) If the whales are lying in very shallow water, try to dig trenches around them to make the water deeper so it will help support their body weight.

Most important of all, *never* try to carry out these emergency procedures yourself without the help of experts. Call local, state, or beach authorities and ask them to contact marine mammal rescuers immediately. People trying to help stranded whales without expert supervision can cause the animals even *worse*, and unnecessary, suffering.

Veterinarian Sweeney   *(Continued on page 97)*

■ *A bottlenose dolphin named Splash is pregnant. She watches, along with trainer Gayle Laule, as Drs. Rae Stone and Jay Sweeney prepare to take a picture of her abdomen, using an ultrasound machine. The ultrasound picture will show how the calf is growing.*

KERBY SMITH

■ *A Commerson's dolphin gives birth to a calf at Sea World in San Diego, California. The calf took 35 minutes to be born, arriving tailfirst. The newborn, named Jacob, quickly surfaced for his first breath with no trouble. He weighed about 20 pounds (9 kg) and measured 2 feet (2/3 m) long. Jacob was the first Commerson's dolphin born in captivity. Scientists hope to breed more of these animals to learn about their growth and behavior. Only two oceanariums have Commerson's dolphins. One is at Sea World of California and one is at the Duisburg Zoo, in West Germany. In the wild, Commerson's dolphins live off the coast of southern South America.*

SEA WORLD PHOTO

■ *A killer whale calf whose mother did not nurse it (left) is fed by Dr. Sweeney, in the sleeveless wet suit, and three staff members at Marineland. They use a pipe with a nipple to feed the calf milk, cream, human infant formula, and vitamins.*

■ *Baby Shamu, a newborn killer whale, swims above her mother (right). Another female follows. Born at Sea World of Florida, Baby Shamu is the first killer whale to be born and to thrive in the care of humans.*

(Continued from page 92) treats stranded animals at the Marineland Animal Center. It is part of Marineland in Los Angeles, California. The center is a clinic for sick or injured animals rescued from beaches near Los Angeles. Many of Dr. Sweeney's patients are seals and sea lions. Others are stranded porpoises and dolphins.

"Most of these animals are very sick and near death by the time they reach the clinic," says Dr. Sweeney. "They may be badly cut and bruised. Sometimes they have worms or broken bones. Our clinic is well equipped to take care of any emergency, even one requiring surgery."

About half the animals that survive are released into the sea. Those that cannot be released are given homes in sea parks if they are healthy enough.

Dr. Sweeney is one of the most highly respected marine mammal veterinarians in the world. In addition to his regular work at the clinic, he travels to many countries to help treat animals.

In 1985, a killer whale was born at Marineland. It weighed 450 pounds (204 kg). The calf's mother did not know how to care for it and did not nurse it. Without food, the baby would die. Dr. Sweeney and other experts quickly began feeding the calf by hand, working day and night.

"We fed the newborn killer whale every six hours," says Brad Andrews, general curator at Marineland. "We gave her a rich blend of milk, whipping cream for extra fat, human baby formula, safflower oil, vitamins, minerals, and extra protein." In spite of all their efforts, the infant killer whale died after 26 days.

Says Dr. Sweeney, "Sometimes it's very hard to save young animals like this one. Without the mother's help in nursing, it is often impossible."

Later in 1985, another killer whale calf was born at Sea World of Florida, in Orlando. That calf's mother accepted it and nursed it. The calf is a little female named Baby Shamu, after her father.

Since birth, Baby Shamu has grown quickly. She now weighs 800 pounds (363 kg). It will be years before she reaches the weight of her mother, some 5,000 pounds (2,268 kg).

Baby Shamu delights visitors at Sea World by appearing in shows with her parents, Shamu and Kandu. Says David Butcher, vice president in charge of animal behavior: "Little Shamu spends a lot of time with the trainers. She exhibits a great deal of curiosity about people. She's getting stronger and more acrobatic as time goes on. Little Shamu seems to enjoy learning to perform."

One of the most important goals of marine parks today is to help animals have healthy young. To do this, parks have well-equipped clinics. By helping marine mammals raise young in captivity, the park staffs can learn much about the animals and their behavior.

The chief veterinarian plays a key role in the operation of any marine park. What is a day like for a marine park vet like Dr. Sweeney?

"Generally, I'll start by walking around the park by 8:30 in the morning, or earlier—before the park opens to the public," says Dr. Sweeney. "I'll look at all the dolphins and other whales, as well as at the seals, sea lions, and elephant seals. I look at their color, expression, weight, behavior, and attitude to see if there are any signs of problems. When the trainers arrive by nine o'clock, they help me and the other veterinarians if we need to treat an animal. For example, we might have to get it out of the water for an exam or for a blood test."

Do the dolphins and other whales at the park get sick often? "No," says Dr. Sweeney. "If they do get sick, it may be something serious, like pneumonia. But that doesn't happen often. We constantly check their health. This process includes giving them

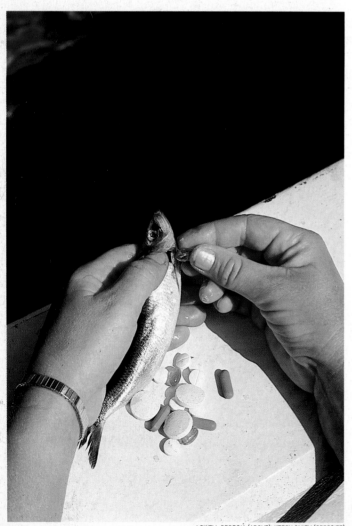

■ *Vitamin pills hidden in the gills of a fish will provide extra nourishment for the dolphin that eats the fish (left). Trainers usually feed vitamin-packed fish to dolphins and other toothed whales in the animals' first meal of the day—when they're hungriest. The whales swallow the food whole. They use their teeth for grasping, not chewing.*

■ *Dr. Sweeney feeds seven-month-old Billy, a bottlenose dolphin, his first fish meal. Billy continues to nurse, but he can now have solid food, too. "Dolphins this age can eat up to four pounds of fish a day," says Dr. Sweeney. Awaiting her turn is Billy's mother, Spray.*

complete physical checkups three times a year."

Caring for toothed whales in captivity requires help from many people—vets, trainers, and other park employees.

Says Dr. Sweeney, "The greatest reward in my job is to walk around the park and see the animals healthy and happy—and to know that I am able to help them be that way."

Animal specialist Gretchen Jacobs of The Living Seas at EPCOT Center says, "I'm glad to think that if dolphins in the wild are ever endangered for some reason, we will have learned enough by working with them and studying them to help save them."

To almost everyone who visits marine parks, dolphins and other toothed whales are special animals. They are loved for their playfulness, beauty, athletic ability, and friendliness.

For me, too, dolphins will always be special. After meeting them and playing with them, I have come to think of them as gentle friends, just as people have for centuries.

Nearly 2,000 years ago, the Greek writer Plutarch said, "To the dolphin alone . . . nature has granted . . . friendship for no advantage." He meant that the dolphin often gave assistance to humans even though it needed no help from them. Today, however, many people *can* share in helping dolphins and other toothed whales—our friends of the sea.

■ *Star performers like these*
bottlenose dolphins named
Chubbs and April seem to
enjoy doing stunts for
people. Here, they "dance"
face to face during a show at
Hawk's Cay Resort, on Duck
Key, Florida. The dolphins
also perform ball tricks,
leaps, flips, and tailwalks—
and they love applause.

INDEX

Library of Congress CIP Data

Rinard, Judith E.
  Dolphins: our friends in the sea.
  (Books for world explorers)
  Bibliography: p.
  Includes index.
  Summary: Discusses dolphins and other toothed whales, both in the wild and in captivity.
  1. Dolphins—Juvenile literature.
  [1. Dolphins. 2. Killer whale. 3. Whales]
  I. Title. II. Title: Dolphins. III. Series.
  QL737.C432R56 1986 599.5'3 86-18126
  ISBN O-87044-609-6 (regular edition)
  ISBN 0-87044-614-2 (library edition)

SOME PLACES TO VISIT TOOTHED WHALES

CALIFORNIA: Marineland, Rancho Palos Verdes; Marine World Africa U.S.A., Vallejo; Sea World, San Diego; Six Flags Magic Mountain, Valencia; Steinhart Aquarium at the Academy of Sciences, San Francisco. **CONNECTICUT:** Friends of the Sea, Enfield; Mystic Marine Life Aquarium, Mystic. **FLORIDA:** Busch Gardens, The Dark Continent, Tampa; Dolphin Research Center, Marathon Shores; Gulfarium, Fort Walton Beach; Gulf World, Panama City Beach; Hawk's Cay Resort & Marina, Marathon; The Living Seas, EPCOT Center, Orlando; Marineland of Florida, St. Augustine; Miami Seaquarium, Key Biscayne; Ocean World, Fort Lauderdale; Sea World of Florida, Orlando; Sugarloaf Lodge, Sugarloaf Key. **HAWAII:** The Kahala Hilton Hotel, Honolulu; Sea Life Park, Makapuu Point, Oahu. **ILLINOIS:** Chicago's Brookfield Zoo, Brookfield. **MARYLAND:** The Jolly Roger Dolphin World, Ocean City; National Aquarium in Baltimore, Baltimore. **MASSACHU-SETTS:** New England Aquarium, Boston; Sealand of Cape Cod, Brewster. **MINNESOTA:** Minnesota Zoological Garden, Apple Valley. **MIS-SISSIPPI:** Marine Life Oceanarium, Gulfport. **NEW YORK:** Aquarium of Niagara Falls, Niagara Falls; New York Aquarium, Brooklyn. **OHIO:** Sea World of Ohio, Aurora. **OKLAHOMA:** Oklahoma City Zoo, Oklahoma City. **PENNSYLVANIA:** The Pittsburgh Zoo, Pittsburgh. **TEXAS:** Sea-Arama Marineworld, Galveston. **VIRGINIA:** Kings Dominion, Doswell. **WASHINGTON:** Point Defiance Zoo & Aquarium, Tacoma. **WISCONSIN:** Milwaukee County Zoological Gardens, Milwaukee. **CANADA:** Sealand of the Pacific, Victoria, British Columbia; Vancouver Aquarium, Vancouver, British Columbia.

DAVID DOUBILET

COVER: *Bottlenose dolphins Chubbs and April relax in their winter home on Duck Key, Florida. During the rest of the year, they perform in shows around the country.*

CONSULTANTS

Thomas J. McIntyre, National Marine Fisheries Service (NOAA), *Chief Consultant*

Glenn O. Blough, LL.D. Emeritus Professor of Education, University of Maryland, *Educational Consultant*

Barbara J. Wood, Montgomery County (Maryland) Public Schools, *Reading Consultant*

Nicholas J. Long, Ph.D., *Consulting Psychologist*

The Special Publications and School Services Division is grateful to the individuals and organizations named or quoted in the text and to those cited here for their generous cooperation during the preparation of *DOLPHINS: OUR FRIENDS IN THE SEA.*

Antony Alpers; Vicki Aversa, National Aquarium in Baltimore; Frank T. Awbrey, Hubbs Marine Research Institute; Lawrence G. Barnes, Natural History Museum of Los Angeles County; Michael A. Bigg, Pacific Biological Station; Deborah Cavanagh, Shelley Kadota, Roy Tanami, Vancouver Aquarium; Holly H. Eby, Sea World of Florida; Pieter A. Folkens, University of California, Santa Cruz; John K. B. Ford, West Coast Whale Research Foundation; Joseph R. Geraci, David St. Aubin, University of Guelph; Louis M. Herman, University of Hawaii; Jackie Hill, Sea World of California; Craig N. McLean, Norman A. Mendes, National Marine Fisheries Service (NOAA); Robert T. Meyer, The Catholic University of America; Alexandra B. Morton; W. Kym Murphy, The Living Seas, EPCOT Center; Catherine T. Payne, Hawk's Cay Resort & Marina; Samuel H. Ridgway, U. S. Naval Ocean Systems Center; Jayne and Mandy Rodriguez, Dolphin Research Center; Jay C. Sweeney; Randall S. Wells, Dolphin Biology Research Associates, Inc.

ADDITIONAL READING

Readers may want to check the *National Geographic Index* and the WORLD Index in a school or a public library for related articles. *Amazing Animals of the Sea—Marine Mammals*, in the National Geographic Society's Books for World Explorers series, and the *National Geographic Book of Mammals* also contain related material. In addition are the following books for young readers ("A" indicates a book for readers at the adult level.): Alpers, Antony, *Dolphins*, John Murray, 1963 (A). Bright, Michael, *Dolphins*, Gallery Books, 1985. Bunting, Eve, *The Sea World of Whales*, Harcourt Brace, Jovanovich, 1980. Caldwell, David K. and Melba C., *The World of the Bottlenosed Dolphin*, J. B. Lippincott Company, 1972. Coffey, David J., *Dolphins, Whales and Porpoises: An Encyclopedia of Sea Mammals*, Collier Books, 1977 (A). Devine, Eleanore, and Martha Clark, *The Dolphin Smile*, Macmillan Publishing Co., Inc., 1967 (A). Hoke, Helen, and Valerie Pitt, *Whales*, Franklin Watts, Inc., 1973. Leatherwood, Stephen, and Randall R. Reeves, *The Sierra Club Handbook of Whales and Dolphins*, Sierra Club, 1983 (A). Marko, Katherine D., *Whales: Giants of the Sea*, Abingdon, 1980. O'Brien, Esse Forrester, *Dolphins: Sea People*, The Naylor Company, 1965. Simon, Seymour, *Killer Whales*, J. B. Lippincott Company, 1978.

Composition for *DOLPHINS: OUR FRIENDS IN THE SEA* by National Geographic's Photographic Services, Carl M. Shrader, Director; Lawrence F. Ludwig, Assistant Director. Printed and bound by Holladay-Tyler Printing Corp., Rockville, Md. Color separations by the Lanman-Progressive Co., Washington, D. C.; NEC, Inc., Nashville, Tenn.

DOLPHINS
Our Friends in the Sea

by Judith E. Rinard

PUBLISHED BY
THE NATIONAL GEOGRAPHIC SOCIETY
WASHINGTON, D. C.

Gilbert M. Grosvenor, *President*
Melvin M. Payne, *Chairman of the Board*
Owen R. Anderson, *Executive Vice President*
Robert L. Breeden, *Senior Vice President*,
Publications and Educational Media

PREPARED BY THE SPECIAL PUBLICATIONS
AND SCHOOL SERVICES DIVISION

Donald J. Crump, *Director*
Philip B. Silcott, *Associate Director*
Bonnie S. Lawrence, *Assistant Director*

BOOKS FOR WORLD EXPLORERS
Pat Robbins, *Editor*
Ralph Gray, *Editor Emeritus*
Ursula Perrin Vosseler, *Art Director*
David P. Johnson, *Illustrations Editor*
Margaret McKelway, *Associate Editor*

STAFF FOR *DOLPHINS: OUR FRIENDS IN THE SEA*
Martha C. Christian, *Managing Editor*
Veronica J. Morrison, *Picture Editor*
Lynette R. Ruschak, *Art Director*
Sheila M. Green, *Researcher*
Patricia N. Holland, *Special Projects Editor*
Joan Hurst, *Editorial Assistant*
Bernadette L. Grigonis, *Illustrations Assistant*
Federico Castelluccio, Pieter A. Folkens,
Marvin J. Fryer, Dorothy Michele Novick, *Artists*
David Street/Streetworks Studio, *Line Art*

ENGRAVING, PRINTING, AND PRODUCT MANUFACTURE: Robert W. Messer, *Manager*; David V. Showers, *Production Manager*; Gregory Storer, Timothy H. Ewing, *Production Project Managers*; George J. Zeller, Jr., *Senior Assistant Production Manager*; Mark R. Dunlevy, *Assistant Production Manager*.

STAFF ASSISTANTS: Vicki L. Broom, Carol R. Curtis, Katherine R. Davenport, Lori Elizabeth Davie, Mary Elizabeth Davis, Ann Di Fiore, Rosamund Garner, Donna L. Hall, Sandra F. Lotterman, Eliza C. Morton, Cleo E. Petroff, Stuart E. Pfitzinger, Nancy J. White, Virginia A. Williams.

MARKET RESEARCH: Mark W. Brown, Joseph S. Fowler, Carrla L. Holmes, Marla Lewis, Barbara Steinwurtzel, Marsha Sussman, Judy Turnbull.

INDEX: Maureen Walsh